FAR WEST

Winner of the L. E. Phillabaum Poetry Award for 2019

POEMS

FAR WEST

Floyd Skloot

LOUISIANA STATE UNIVERSITY PRESS ▌▌ BATON ROUGE

Published by Louisiana State University Press
Copyright © 2019 by Floyd Skloot
All rights reserved
Manufactured in the United States of America
LSU Press Paperback Original
First printing

Designer: Barbara Neely Bourgoyne
Typeface: Whitman
Printer and binder: LSI

Cataloging-in-Publication Data are available from the Library of Congress.

ISBN 978-0-8071-7202-9 (pbk.: alk. paper) — ISBN 978-0-8071-7187-5 (pdf) —
ISBN 978-0-8071-7188-2 (epub)

For Beverly

CONTENTS

III.

IV.

ACKNOWLEDGMENTS

These poems were previously published in the following journals, sometimes in different forms: *American Journal of Poetry*: "Chris Cagle Is Dead," "Coconut Patties," "Over and Over," and "Visit"; *Hopkins Review*: "Fever Dream," "The Finish," "Holiday," "Jet Song," and "Zoot Suit"; *Hudson Review*: "The Discovery"; *HU: The Honest Ulsterman* (UK): "The Scat Singer, 1958"; *Miramar*: "Headland Walk, Cornwall"; *New World Writing*: "Harvest Moon, Manzanita, Oregon" and "Simple Gifts"; *Notre Dame Review*: "The Birthday Gift, 1955"; *Oregon English Journal*: "The Scat Singer, 1958"; *Plume*: "At Last," "Congregation," "The Family Plot," and "The Master Bird"; *Poem Magazine* (England): "A Season of Killdeer"; *Poetry Daily*: "City Championship, 1926"; *Poetry Northwest*: "Peacock at Tule Springs"; *Prairie Schooner*: "The Lost Name," "No Wake Zone," and "Tangled"; *Sewanee Review*: "Island," "Jules Verne at Safeco Field, Seattle, Spring 2014," "Life Bird," "Memento," "A Season of Killdeer," and "Sky Dance"; *Southern Review*: "Childe Hassam at the Oregon Coast, Summer 1904," "Nabokov in Goal, Cambridge, 1919," "Sabbath," and "*Yahrzeit*"; *Southern Poetry Review*: "City Championship, 1926," "Thomas Hardy and Rudyard Kipling Househunting, September 1897," and "Yesternight in Elsinore"; *Tar River Poetry*: "The Scat Singer, 1958"; *Valparaiso Poetry Review*: "Sock Basketball"; *Zyzzyva*: "Schumann in Düsseldorf, 1854."

I am grateful for the help of my wife, Beverly Hallberg, first reader of these poems, and for the insight and comments provided by my friend Ron Slate, who also read drafts of each of these poems.

I.

THE LOST NAME

One day this fall I could not remember
the name of the island in Hawaii
where we'd spent a week in December.
There was a wall around the word.

I closed my eyes. Then I thought
of the red-crested cardinal who kept
returning to our lanai, the yellow tang
ablaze in the reef as sunlight swept

through a quick break of cloud, the sprawling
banyan tree near Lahaina Harbor. Names
everywhere in my brain, nerve cells sparkling
with names. Crimson opakapaka came

to mind. Haleakala. Snorkel Bob's.
But not the island. Not the sound
of it, not even the first letter. If I let
go, thought of something else, looked around,

it might come to me. I knew I could open
Rand McNally, check online, ask my wife.
Green turtles and breaching humpback whales.
Cattle egret glimpsed in the blink of an eye.

TANGLED

He's that actor you don't remember
from the movie you've seen a dozen times
or more. In the background, maybe "September
Song" but you can't be sure. Was he in the scene
on an island drenched in reds and green,
angles widening as morning sun climbs
above the trees and in a heartbeat fades
into mist? He has the soft voice you hear
only later, outside, sounding the way blades
of grass look to you when autumn skies clear.
What was it he whispered? All that remains
is the whisper itself tangled in notes
from some other song. Its melody floats
now just beyond the sound made by two skeins
of Canada geese coming together,
gathering to face the heavy weather.

OVER AND OVER

My brain is a jukebox stuffed with old songs
playing a phrase or two at random over
and over. I keep the volume turned low
but you can sometimes see my lips move
as I sing along, eyebrows rising as I reach
for a silent high note. If you asked me
whether I know the lyrics to "Over and Over"
I would say *No* and blame it on being
past seventy, then find the song
repeating in my head an hour later as I fold
the laundry. Bobby Day,1958, B-side
of "Rockin' Robin." I'm eleven and listening
to my brother's 45s before he gets home
from school. *I went to a dance the other night.*
Everybody went stag. Also late 1965,
the Dave Clark Five. *I said over and over*
and over again this dance is gonna be
a drag. I'll hear both versions off and on
for hours till someone says *wasn't it awful*
about the tanker fire yesterday morning?
and then I'll hear the soft piano and drums
opening into "Smoke Gets In Your Eyes."
They asked me how I knew. I don't know
how I still know these lyrics. Haven't thought
of them in fifty years at least. The Platters,
Nat King Cole, Eartha Kitt. Just a boy.
But now the lines repeat and expand, melody
and rhyme tricky, *When your heart's on fire,*
you must realize, all the way to dinnertime
when I start preparing trout with lime, cilantro

and coconut. That unleashes Harry Nilsson
singing *put the lime in the coconut,* the only
phrase I know from his song. I'm not even sure
I've heard "Coconut" from beginning to end
but those six words repeat over and over
till now, just thinking *over and over* again,
there it is: *I went to a dance the other night.*

JET SONG

—West Side Story, *August 1962*

As soon as we were sure we knew the dance
the choreographer changed it. Instead
of jumping onto the bench from stage left,
leap over it from behind. Can you lift
your arms as you land? Riff and A-rab, thread
your way through that line of trash bins, and glance
at each other when you sing the word *Jet*.
Let's have you start to spin on *cigarette*.
I can hear her smoke-scorched voice even now
urging us to reach for the sky on our last
dying day. Move as one. You are a gang!
In the echoing space the mirrored room sang
our songs back on us. Don't twirl, try a fast
fan kick and when you hunch and snap, stay low.
Forget the very idea of steps but be
sure you remember the steps themselves—free
yourselves to move the music among you
so your bodies contain the whole story
in each step, and the dancing will be true.

CHRIS CAGLE IS DEAD

1955

I spread my old-time All-American
football cards in T-formation
on my parents' bedroom floor as they dress
for dinner with friends.
Now playing quarterback:
Little Frankie Albert!
He throws a pass into the hall
where Bill Daddio makes a leaping catch
and laterals to Choo-Choo Charlie Justice
by the antique chest of drawers!

I love to say the players' names
and sometimes if he's in a good mood
ask my father what they do now.
He always knows.
Whizzer White is a lawyer
and *Johnny Lujack sells Chevys.*
Beattie Feathers is a coach down south.
Cotton Warburton makes movies in Hollywood.

But tonight my father paces while he ties
and re-ties his Windsor knot,
no longer even speaking to my mother
about how late
she will make them again.
He stops long enough to find
his cufflinks, rattles them like dice in his palm.

My mother lights
another Chesterfield and glares
at him in her mirror. So I begin
picking up my cards.
As my father passes, I reach out
to show him my new favorite.
He slaps it to the floor.
Chris Cagle is dead.

*

1929

The back of his card says he was a bolt
of lightning: Fast, dangerous, Army's best
broken field runner ever. Nicknamed *Red*,
the fiery Cagle thought a helmet slowed
him down. If he had to wear one, he kept
the chin strap loose. Loved to hit and be hit.

*

1961

I still don't know where I am.
I still don't know what happened
but my brother says he'll give me
another concussion if I ask again.

It's dark and he's in his bed
watching *Have Gun—Will Travel*.
I can't imagine how
it could be Saturday night.

My head hurts.
There's a scab forming on my lower lip
in the shape of my upper teeth.
There are too many pillows on my bed.

The last thing I remember
is returning to the school bus
because we'd come to the wrong field.
No marching band, no fans, no opponents.
I shuffle among my teammates in our dark
blue uniforms, wind whishing through
my helmet's ear holes, cleats clattering
across the blacktop. Then the bus starts

and I wake up in my bed
across the room from my brother
unable to decide if the sound
of gunfire comes from the television
or inside my head. My brother looks
at me, sighs and agrees
to tell me what happened
one last time.

He says I took a hard hit to the head
returning the opening kickoff
and later in the quarter made open
field tackles on four straight plays.
From the bleachers he could see
I was woozier after each play,
staggering back to my position, shaking
my head. He was making his way
down to alert the coach
as the fifth play began.
He says he vaulted the fence

and ran to me. He says he covered
my convulsing body with his.

*

1963

I sit on a bench in the locker room
wrapping my ankles in tape.
Then I step into a girdle of hip
and tailbone pads, lacing them tight.
I slip thigh and knee pads into slots
on my pants, then reach my arms
through straps on shoulder pads,
and adjust a pair of elbow pads.
I put on my helmet, snap the chin strap,
adjust the face mask, stuff a mouth guard
in place. Beside me, my best friend
Jay slaps the sides and top of my helmet
bing bang boom and we walk
toward Saturday morning light
funneling through the field house doors.

I remember the whistle blew the play dead.
I remember stopping beside a pile
of players at midfield and then I remember
waking up on the ground without feeling
in my fingers or toes. I wanted to get up.
The referee began blowing his whistle again,
screaming *late hit late hit* as he threw down
a penalty flag and Jay knelt beside me.
I remember his helmet coming into view,
black stripes under his eyes and his voice
telling me not to move.

My mother said *If your father were alive*
to see this again. She said *that first time*
he had nightmares you'd be a vegetable
the rest of your life, God forbid. She didn't say
I killed him with worry but she might as well.
You, young man, are lucky to be alive.

Next year, she tore up the permission form.
No more football! I spent that season
working in a butcher's freezer cutting beef
and pork I'd hauled from delivery trucks,
pretending I was tackling them for a loss.

*

1942

The night after Christmas, two men found
Cagle on hands and knees at the bottom
of a staircase in the Broadway-Nassau
subway station. He said his head hurt.

He was thirty-seven but looked fifty
as he sat between them on the train,
sober but slurring his words, telling them
every time the car rocked it seemed
he was being kicked in the head.

The next morning his wife took him
to the hospital. Cause of death:
laceration of the brain and a bruise
of the tissues on both sides of the brain.

*

2016

It's been twenty-eight years
since a neuro-virus found my brain
open to attack. My doctors say
with my history I'm lucky the cognitive
damage is no worse. Lucky to be alive.
When I first saw the scans I thought
my brain looked like cleat-pocked dirt.
At least once a year I dream
I'm standing alone near our end zone
waiting for the kickoff, and the ball
has been tumbling toward me for years
through the air, and I'm aware of my brain
within my skull within my helmet
seeming to throb with knowledge of what
is about to happen as I cradle the ball
at last and begin to run into the fall wind.

THE DISCOVERY

Because of the sketch's colors and shapes,
because the artist was burly and spoke
with a Spanish accent, wore a beret
and sandals, head wreathed in cigarette smoke,
because the Brooklyn street corner that day
should have been Paris before the war broke
out, my mother knew she had bought a work
by Picasso's secret son. She would say
his name, Raul, and point out the quick strokes
of his half-hidden initials, the way
they were part of a crescent form that may
or may not have been his father's curved back
etched in the boy's mind. Finding it was fate,
pure and simple, the rarest kind of luck,
and the tones went perfectly with our drapes.

AT LAST

—for my brother

We could have finished our ongoing game
of *Careers* abandoned in early1964
after your tenth trip to the moon.
We could have kept singing the score
of *Kismet* from "Fate" to "Sands of Time"
till we sounded effortless on the harmonies.
We could have remembered the setups
to this scribbled list of punchlines I just found
in a file labeled PHILIP JOKES and we could
have continued our discussion of whether
La Serenata served better clams oreganata
than Mario's before the old chef retired,
whether ham was better eaten hot or cold,
frankfurters with sauerkraut or cole slaw.
We could have settled whether Dean Martin
was better with or without Jerry Lewis
and which Everly Brother was the heart
of the act. I could have gone to Vegas
with you as you wished before you lost
your sight, before you could no longer walk,
before the years of dialysis, and we could
have seen the latest Elvis. I could have learned
to play pai gow poker, your favorite,
and nursed one rye and ginger till our luck
turned. Then we could have shared a room
again after all these years and as we fell asleep
I could have told you of our mother's funeral
nine years after yours, her rages lost at last

in thick clusters and tangles of dementia,
her smile and voice equal parts you and me,
calm as the desert night, an ending I felt
neither of us could possibly have imagined.

PEACOCK AT TULE SPRINGS

—Las Vegas, Nevada

In the late autumn dust and constant wail
of two seed-scattering tractors I thought
the bolt of blue before me on the trail
was a broken bottle until I caught
movement out of the corner of my eye.
I thought it might be blowing leaves
till it rose and slowly unfolded in waves
of sudden color as the cloudy sky
cleared. His tail became a curtain
parting and I saw my daughter beside
me at dusk in a South Carolina park
forty years ago. She was laughing, certain
the peacock calling from the dark
edge of woods knew he did not need to hide
from her. She held my hand as he emerged
into what was left of the day's light.
I could hear and feel how her breath surged
and she whispered *I knew I was right.*

THE FINISH

In this last half-mile of the longest race
I have ever run the road curves to face
the late afternoon sun and starts a steep
climb. I lean into the hill and try to keep
my pace steady. All I can see ahead
is glare off the dark surface of the road
and pine trees thinning. All I can hear
is the slap of my footfall and the flare
of my breath though I try to control it,
knowing if I don't I'll have nothing left
long before I reach the invisible crest.

FEVER DREAM

I had my moment in the afterlife,
faced the all-consuming white light
and began the motionless dance
to a music that was more warmth
than sound. From the dark place
below I thought someone said
I was beyond reach. Yet peace
in the form of breath that was not
my own suffused my body, absorbing
the last vestiges of pain. The way back
grew narrower than the way ahead.
But then I heard the one voice
I would never stop turning to.
She called my name and I went to her.

YESTERNIGHT IN ELSINORE

> My lord, I think I saw him yesternight.
> —HORATIO TO HAMLET, Act 1, Scene 2

For days since the King's funeral and Queen's
remarriage, Horatio kept his uneasy distance,
not letting Hamlet know he was in Elsinore,
maintaining a watch on his grieving friend.

It troubled him to observe the always graceful
Hamlet move as though in a formal dance
as the new King's reign began. Troubled him
to see his friend's empty smile and rigid carriage,
the courtly correctness as he endured
those awful ceremonies. Horatio knew
there would be time later, back at Wittenberg,
to speak the words of true consolation
it was too soon now for Hamlet to hear.

But then the two sentinels came at dawn,
breathless, frightened as Horatio had never
known them to be, whispering of the dead
King returned to Elsinore. Twice now during
their watch and close enough to touch if
they dared. He'd been certain it was nothing
but their middle-of-the-night fantasies
till he faced the thing himself, saw sorrow
in its countenance, and watched it drift
within the predawn mist, armored,
elusive as breath in the cold air.

Reason fails when a man of reason stands
before a ghost. Having seen the King alive,
recognized him in Hamlet all their days together,
he had no doubt who the ghost had been,
or how its voice would sound if it had spoken
in those last moments before the cock crowed.

Horatio could feel time as he understood it
stop. He tried to think as he had been trained
to think at Wittenberg. If the ghost could walk
the ramparts, why did it not enter the castle?
Why not speak? Love and duty told Horatio
how he must act. But knowing Hamlet's quicksilver
moods, he could foresee what this formless vision
would do to him. He feared bearing the news
as deeply as he feared the news itself.

As so often at school, Hamlet would be lost
to himself. He would need Horatio beside him
through the sleepless hours, the ceaseless
pacing and muttering to himself—eyes bloodshot
and jittering—the wit sharpened against
no one more than himself. They would
walk the familiar landscape as Hamlet
tried to reason his way to clarity, slow the rush
of conclusion. But he would believe
that his father's restless spirit had come
loose from the afterworld, had come back
so that Hamlet could help him find peace.
There would be no rest in this life
or the next till he understood why.

At least, Horatio knew, there was no
violence in Hamlet's scholarly soul.
This he believed beyond doubt. It freed
him to rush off and find his friend at last,
certain they would get through this together.

II.

NABOKOV IN GOAL, CAMBRIDGE, 1919

> I was crazy about goal keeping.
> —VLADIMIR NABOKOV, *Speak, Memory*

He loved to lose himself in the game
opening before him. Breath slowed
as play flowed and he fluttered
in the goal, adjusting socks, knee
guards, gloves, cap. Body checkered
by the net's shadow, he anticipated
angles of attack and grew
calmer as the action approached.

When the ball was downfield
he leaned against a post and closed
his eyes sometimes, knowing
teammates' positions by their calls
and cries. Nabokov spoke so many
tongues that he rejoiced then
in the plain sounds of a kicked ball,
savored the nuance of a foot's impact
on leather. There was also wind
to read, light to keep track of
and the softening autumn grass
turning to mud at midfield.

Nothing that held still was of interest
as he shifted within the goal, aware
but not aware of poems taking shape
in his mind tuned now to no language
ever known. This was the moment

of being lost. He rode its rhythms
long enough to soar across the goal
and catch a shot as it spun and dove
on the arc of its own sizzling flight.

JULES VERNE AT SAFECO FIELD, SEATTLE, SPRING 2014

On his deathbed Verne vowed to return
in a hundred years. That he is nine years
late he attributes to the way time skews
in the afterlife. That he is in Seattle
instead of Amiens he attributes to the uneven
rush and spin of Earth among the spheres.
The rain he recognizes as a seaport rain,
fine and briny in the early afternoon,
with the screech of gulls borne on gusty
west winds. Foghorns blare in the harbor,
as familiar to him as his own lost breath.
He savors firm ground beneath his feet.

He had foreseen raised roadways curving
over other roadways, skyscrapers with their
structures fully exposed, aircraft that whirl
and hover, that rise straight into the sky.
So too the cacophony of giant machines,
dense smell of fuels, rubble fields clogging
the heart of the city, sleek vessels
skimming above the water's rough surface.

But to see it all at once, to sense its
energy flowing through him, surpasses
his wildest imaginings. He is light
with the pleasure of it, yet he knows
he has come back for more than this,
more than confirmation of his vision
of a changing world. Pounding music mixed

with spoken song cascades around him
from somewhere he cannot determine.
Voices are everywhere, people talking
to the air as they pass through it, gesturing,
colliding, eyes focused wholly inward.
The atmosphere is alive with pulsing colors.

He stands beneath a double-decked
bridge of bright black steel and feels
the current of bodies sweeping past.
He has missed this movement of a crowd.
It carries him inside a vast concrete
arena blazing under strange white lights.
Maybe five hundred lights stacked
almost to the arched roof, far too bright
for his eyes to look at but spellbinding
in their steady otherworldly glow.
Row after row of seats overlook a bowl
of the greenest grass he has ever seen.

He tries to remain in place. The wind
and rain are dwindling as he looks
through walls that are not there,
that are nothing but crossed trusses
and silvering sky open to the elements
though there is a roof afloat above.

Now daylight begins to drift over the field,
its progress slow enough to doubt it is
happening until he turns his gaze upwards.
The roof appears to be folding back into itself
like a telescope. This is something he had
not foreseen! He falls back into a seat

and watches the roof opening millimeter
by millimeter. He thinks it is like one layer
of heaven pulling back to reveal
a deeper heaven. As it opens, the sun begins
to leave the cover of a cloud and he is
bathed in its slow forgotten warmth.

CHILDE HASSAM AT THE OREGON COAST, SUMMER 1904

He woke in the sand and grass of a dune
on Cannon Beach, close to the rocky cove
where he'd worked till dark. Rolling surf
was the sound of pain deep in his head.

Even with his eyes closed he could still
see line after line of foaming breakers
from horizon to shore, cerulean and violet
with hidden life. Everything moved
quickly here at the edge—light, surface
texture, the shapes of land and sea,
structure of cloud. It demanded speed
in return, an art of the moment.

He could not keep up with what he saw.
Flocks of tufted puffins soaring south
toward the sea stacks were lost before
he could move his hand. The flicker
of backlit spume against broken clamshells
eluded him. He was too slow for brown
pelicans' small shifts against sudden gusts
or the touch and go of pelagic cormorants.

But in late afternoon he'd finally felt his limbs
loosen, sensed the day's heat softening
his body from the outside in. When it came,
sleep was a sudden plunge. Dreams swirled
within cyclones of unstable forms and tones.

Now he stood, feeling salt spray soak his scalp,
and turned his back on the incoming tide
to see the sun rise over the Coast Range
as through a scrim of western tanager feathers.

At first he thought his cornea must be scored
by wind-blown grit or his vision somehow
tinged by the turbulent moods that returned
with the solstice and drove him out of Boston,

exhausted, unable to think or feel, absorbed
by wayward thoughts. He blinked but the strange
sight remained, so he knew this red drenched
in orange, this wild yellow wash and coal
black border borrowed from the bird's wings
were exactly what he'd been missing,
what he'd traveled this far west to find.

SCHUMANN IN DÜSSELDORF, 1854

In the middle of a long winter night
Schumann stands by his flickering window
and listens to heaven's harmonies fall.
They are disguised as windblown snow
but he can hear their frail mystery, bright
music transformed by hidden moonlight.
All his senses waken to the secret storm.
Its imminence has kept him from sleep for weeks.
Snowflakes are winter butterflies, trees dance
to take the place of dreams that have gone
from him, and hints of new melodic forms leak
through thin panes. Angels come to glance
at his blank manuscript pages, to hear
his unwritten melodies and tell
him snowdrifts are not white devils after all
nor is the wind a tiger roaring in his inner ear.

THOMAS HARDY AND RUDYARD KIPLING
HOUSEHUNTING, SEPTEMBER 1897

Up early, Hardy hears his young friend
already outside and marching through
fallen leaves, declaiming in his slender
voice to the eager dog barking beside him.
Redstarts call from the front hedges,
blackcaps from the line of beech trees,
lesser whitethroat from the berry bushes
where they stop on their way south.
Everything planted by Hardy's own hands
around this house he designed and built.

He walks to the window and looks
through fading darkness, glad to know
which birds are there this close to equinox.
But he's not sure how he would feel
if the Kiplings were to settle nearby, so loud
and full of family life. Perhaps the men
will fail in their searches again today.

Hardy dresses in his old tweed cycling suit
with the thick stockings and double-seated
knickers the maid darned after his latest
fall coming home from Sherborne in June.
He pauses and thinks of the solo osprey
chanced upon yesterday as they crested
a slow hill not far from the sea. A male,
fattened for long flight. It was gone
before he could call it to Kipling's attention
without interrupting the miles-long monologue.

Today promises to be another good day
to cycle Dorset, this time to Weymouth,
provided Kipling doesn't speak of politics
or war or the burden of a growing family.
Or the club in London, or publishers in America,
gossip about Henry James, Mark Twain.
They plan to see a house at Rodwell
and some land on top of the Ridgeway.
Hardy warned him this was much too close
to the guns firing off Portland, and Kipling
replied that he would particularly like that.
Yes, perhaps nothing will quite satisfy him
and there will be only the search to savor.

Hardy buttons his baggy waistcoat, knots
his tie, the soft stained gloves Emma bought
him when they first began riding together.
He feels younger now, at fifty-seven, finished
with writing novels, solely a poet for the rest
of his life, free to follow his passion for cycling.
At the front door he puts on his new Panama
hat and horse-skin North Road shoes, scuffing
them in the dust while he leans against
his beloved low-slung Rover Cob and waits
for Kipling in a beam of morning sun.

*

Kipling turns back toward the house and sees
Hardy waiting in a beam of morning sun.
There is something like a smile beneath
his ragged gray moustache and—at ease
beside his bicycle—from this angle he seems

a kind and gentle soul at peace with the world.
But the looming house is a cheerless and grim
brick fortress behind dull brick walls and tall
trees that seal the place off from light as well
as intruders. This is just about as Kipling imagined,
a home as dark as Hardy's shielded heart.

At thirty-one, he has traveled far more
of the world than Hardy. India, Rangoon,
Hong Kong, San Francisco, Victoria, Boston,
Niagara Falls. The idea of home has become
so elusive he wonders if it's just another way
of thinking about God. A hopeless quest.
This is nothing he has ever spoken of,
not even to Carrie, whom he married five
years ago and took immediately to Vermont
and Yokohama. Back in London for a year,
blessed now with a son, he doesn't know
if he wants to find a house in this sparse
landscape where everything feels like
a chapter in a novel by his aging friend.
Besides, he dreams about the maple trees
in New England and is planning a winter
visit to South Africa this year or next.

It takes all morning to cover the ten miles
south toward Wyke Regis and the sea.
Kipling is thinking of stories he hopes
to write for little children and of lines
in his poem for the Queen's Jubilee
that could have been improved if he'd had
more time. Hardy shows him an ancient
hill fort near Winterborne Monkton, a church

in Bincombe with a view of Coombe Valley
and the Channel, the square where
he'd set a story more than a decade ago.

At a house near the shore of Portland Harbor
Kipling begins to read the lease and shakes
his head. *No,* he whispers, and Hardy
understands. Kipling cannot tie himself
to a property in this part of the world.

Hardy informs the owner that this is
Mr. Rudyard Kipling, the acclaimed author,
Kipling introduces Hardy as the great poet
and novelist from Dorset, and she tells them
she has never heard of them. At the water's
edge they share a last flask of tea.

III.

YAHRZEIT

My father died at fifty-three
fifty-three years ago today.

I remember that the morning
after my daughter was born
in the middle of a long September night
my mother responded to the news
by telling me I had been born
in the middle of an even longer night

and on that night my father drove
home from the hospital, lit a cigar
and climbed out the living
room window. He sat on the fire
escape in the company of a dozen
pigeons and finished his fifth
of Cutty Sark and sack of salted filberts.

This was the rare story my mother
told about him that I could
verify because our former neighbor
from the apartment below sent
an email confirming it. For hours,
while she and her parents lay awake,
my father's feet kept time against
the metal ladder just above them
as he sang "Flat Foot Floogie
(with the Floy Floy)" over and over,
surely in honor of my strange first name.

*

I was named for Flora, my mother's
grandmother. "Flat Foot Floogie
(with the Floy Floy)" was a jazz song
written nine years before I was born,
the year my parents married. The most
common explanation of the title
is that Floy Floy is slang for
a venereal disease and Floogie
really means Floozie. My father
often sang this song while dressing
to go out for dinner with my mother,
his way of making me laugh before
they left. I believe my father
understood what the song was about
but had chosen not to argue
with my mother over yet another
point of contention regarding this child
he never wanted. And whenever he sang
it, I would laugh and my mother
would stalk out of the room.

*

My mother told me
without quite telling me
that my father wanted me
aborted. He knew people, she said.
The mob controlled Red Hook
where he operated his chicken
market, so he knew people.
Italian butchers and bakers

on either side of him. The squeeze,
she said. What did I think,
he got by because he was
a nice guy? Protection money,
the rackets, fix anything,
back room, back alley, back door.
He knew people, my mother told me.

*

I was fourteen when he died
so I have now lived fourteen
years longer than he lived.

Half a year ago, an elderly physician
from New York who as a young man
delivered crates of live poultry to
my father's market in the early 1950s
called to say he was going through
old boxes as he prepared to move
into a retirement community and found
a photograph of my father holding
me in his arms in the courtyard
of our Flatbush apartment building.
He wanted to tell me something
important before he sent the picture:
My father was a lovely man.
And he was so proud of me
because I could recite the entire
Brooklyn Dodgers' lineup, including
uniform numbers and positions,
when I was three years old.

*

I no longer remember the sound
of his voice. I have forgotten how
he laughed. Photos show him
with more hair than I remember,
an actual smile, more weight,
fewer wrinkles on his face, eyeglasses
always held in his hand when posing.
I no longer remember anything
about him that I have not already
remembered. Almost all who knew
him are gone. If he was still alive
he would be one hundred six.

CITY CHAMPIONSHIP, 1926

My father was a sprinter in his youth
nicknamed Horse for the hitch in his gait.
Here he is airborne in a mid-stride haze.
His singlet ripples in the wind, his face
calmer than I remember it even in sleep
as he reaches through air and its currents
part for him. His body knows the plain truth
of pure speed and all he needs to do is keep
going as he is, ablaze in the afternoon light.

ZOOT SUIT

For my sixth birthday, I wanted a zoot
suit, whatever that was. Sounded sharp,
crisp, all snazzy creases and fat stripes,
a fast set of clothes that rhymed with Skloot.

No toys. No games. Nothing else would do.
Yes, I would be away at summer camp
and not need a suit. Yes, a Sunday trip
to Ebbets Field to see the Dodgers play two
against the Giants had been on my list.

But that was before I heard about zoot
suits. Just saying the words aloud was good,
and I would laugh to myself as I wished
for two, maybe three, red and blue and green.
They sounded like they were already mine.

SOCK BASKETBALL

A bottomless, lidless shoebox
taped above my bedroom door
became the hoop, with a pair
of rolled-up socks as the ball.

I was preparing for the growth
spurt that never arrived. Slam
dunk, spin moves, sky hook,
fingertips against the ceiling.

Game after game as the clock
ticked the last seconds down
the score was tied, the crowd
went wild. I stood in the light

from a window, ball in hand,
only a bed and burly chest
of drawers between me and
victory, calm in the knowledge

that in this tight space I had all
the moves, the perfect touch.

THE SCAT SINGER, 1958

In the cellar at night my father beat
the speed-bag till its sound blurred
into a bass line. I heard him singing
nonsense syllables against a patch
of melody made up as he went along.
Sometimes he sounded like himself
at prayer, when mumbled Hebrew
rose and fell with the flicker of light,
and there were times he sounded
like God answering that prayer.
Sometimes he seemed to solo
around the memory of mother's
piano riffs lingering from late
afternoon. Down in the dark was
his only tuneful place, and deep
in the night I could believe his steady
song would keep us all safe.

HOLIDAY

If he had lived one more day
my father might have risen
at dawn to walk as he had not
in years, heedless, free of pain.
After the best sleep in memory,
he might have seen a Sunday
unlike any he had seen before,
scored to the sighing whistle
of cedar waxwings hidden
in a mountain ash he passed
along the trail. He might have
had time for another ride on
the roan quarter horse followed
by a dozen laps in the pool.
He might have called me
and I would have come to him
though I was on an island
a hundred miles away, a boy
of fourteen, asleep still
in the day's new light.

VISIT

In early spring I dream her last
months again. I enter the secret
code, then follow the long gleaming
hallway as the doors close and lock
behind us. There is the man holding
a stuffed brown bear and babbling
in his wheelchair. The nurses' aide
pats a blank-faced woman shrieking
as she nears her room. In the sunlit
distance, the solarium where my mother
sits beside a bowl of boiled eggs.
Her softened voice is no longer
the voice of rage. Her livid eyes
are nearly sightless now, the teeth
that bit her own fist in fury are gone.

Her questions are always the same:
Am I married? Are you married?
Are we married? Soon she sings
a phrase or two, drifts into pure
melody, fades toward silence
and slowing breath, closes her eyes,
sleeps. When I begin to sing her song
she nods and smiles but does not wake.
I wonder if her ravaged brain
allows her still to dream and would
those dreams be of gleaming
hallways, locked doors, wild screams?
Would she be free of all the forces
that haunted her before, that haunted
us all who lived in her terrible thrall?

MEMENTO

I remember she told me it was a rock
taken from the yard of the family home
on the day they fled Bialystok,
a reminder of what we have come from.
One look and she could smell the forest air,
see distant treetops, hear chickens in their coops,
women's voices in the street, the men at prayer,
the time before the coming of the troops.

I remember she told me it was a stone
taken from the camel path on Mount Sinai,
sacred, the color of God's breath, of bone,
an endless blessing on the whole family
back to the very beginning of time.

I remember she told me it was a pebble
from the giant mountain of boulders piled
at the edge of my grandfather's village, rubble
the Cossacks left behind. Maybe a piece
of the bakery, temple, butcher shop.

I remember it was always there but each
time it was a different size and shape.
The last time I saw it was a week after
she died and in dim light through her lace
curtains as the afternoon grew darker
I thought it looked exactly like her voice.

SABBATH

My grandmother brought the old country back
to her Brooklyn kitchen by Sabbath candlelight.
She refused to wait for sundown. I heard trolley
cars squealing on their tracks, the hiss of buses
braking, car horns, and neighbors chattering
behind the steady beat of her half-moon blade
as she chopped livers and onions still slick
with chicken fat from a jar on her windowsill.
She held the shallow wooden bowl snug
between her arm and ribs, flickering light caught
in her blade. My job was to bring boiled eggs
from the icebox and—when she nodded—toss
them into her bowl with a fist of salt and pepper
from the cracked dish her own mother used.

THE BIRTHDAY GIFT, 1955

My furrier grandfather cut a pink
mink bicycle seat cover with matching
handlebar grips for my eighth birthday.
They came tucked in golden tissue paper
inside a cardboard box wrapped with silver
foil by my mother and topped with eight small
sea green bows. Since my bike had been stolen
half a year ago I thought the gift meant
a new one must be hidden somewhere in
our apartment. I was giddy as I ran
from room to room, opening closet doors,
looking for a chain and lock, a bell,
a light that would flash when I pedaled,
knowing before I returned to the living
room that there was nothing more to be found.

COCONUT PATTIES

My grandparents were a box of coconut
patties brought back from Miami in February
just for me. They were a tiny kitchen reeking
of flanken and roasted root vegetables,
a samovar of tea, rugelach from the bakery
around the corner. His laugh was the roar
of an airplane propeller and hers was silent
but made her bounce. Always a short sashay
to Central Park and back at dusk followed by
a game of gin rummy on the living room sofa
while traffic rattled the apartment's windows.
When they spoke of the old country—*Krakow!
Tuchow!*—they spit three times over their shoulders
to ward off the evil eye and kissed their fingertips.

ISLAND

My father was a man of winter night.
He was early darkness, sharp winds, black ice
on the last curve home, and sudden strange light
from a Full Wolf Moon when it starts to rise.
My mother was a woman of force twelve
winds out of nowhere. She was huge waves, air
filled with driving spray, storm feeding on itself
and hurling debris as it hovered there,
a mass of fury, unable to move.
We lived on an island with no bridges
left standing. The mainland was lost in mist
most of the time or glimpsed at the edges
of sight for a second, gaudy as a wish,
out of place, still as nothing else I knew.

THE FAMILY PLOT

Through shadows I can see my brother
sink down on his knees, lost in prayer.
Even as it happens I know it could never
happen. Then he is holding the sphinx pose,
doing yoga to welcome solstice. So now
I realize my brother can only be me,
half my age and halfway through a set
of diamond pushups, each one slow
enough to seem like stillness from this
distance. We are in front of an old oak
and the hedge lurking beside us turns
into our parents, angry voices caught
within the hissing wind. Before us all
tombstones tilt in the rain-softened earth.

IV.

THE MASTER BIRD

Among the warblers in our woods was one
that spring we thought of as the master bird.
His voice, pitched high against the rising sun
as though to stall it, seemed to be what stirred
the others into song. A soloist
of dawn, his full golden breast matched the light
that fractured in its passage through chaste twists
of oak and maple. He gave us one bright
moment of melody to remember,
then was swallowed by the day. But we'd caught
his act. That pure voice was the November
harbored in every March, the death held taut
in every birth. It aired the theme for all
the rest to use in answer to his call.

HEADLAND WALK, CORNWALL

The footpath leads us through an open gate
to sandy grassland flecked with Queen Anne's lace.
Silver-studded blue butterflies flicker
around us as we reach the bluff and face
a sea that seems to drain the sky of light.
Near the edge, the warm spring air grows thicker.
The cove unfolds its arms of layered slate
and fulmar circle below us, flashing white.

After the long day's drive from Western Wales
it is the space that claims us now. This field
in a few weeks will burst into the red
and yellow of poppy and marigold,
but now it wraps us in its firm green hold.
We breathe deep as the evening wind swells.

LIFE BIRD

—*Wadsworth Wetlands, Lake County, Illinois*

Two old men at the far edge
of the marsh look back at us
through binoculars as we look
at them through binoculars.

Blurred a few yards behind,
a third person turns into
a rolling luggage rack
rigged with camera gear
as I bring him into focus.

We have all come in search
of the same furtive little bird
seen here earlier this morning,
a Least Bittern walking on lily
leaves in the thick August light.
Word went out online and we
have driven fifty miles to add
the Least to my wife's life list.

As the men begin to scan
the shore we hear a harsh
and raspy *wak wak wak*
that means the bird is nearby.
All we can see in the still
water are reeds and bunched
leaves from the place we heard
the call, but the men, crouched
together, have seen something.

We walk the arc of a narrow
path toward them, keeping to
the margins, keeping quiet.
As one man sets up a tripod
the other whispers their welcome
and leads my wife to a spongy
knob of shoreline. He points,
checks his watch, steps back,
and she lifts her binoculars,
breathing deep to steady herself.

The Least Bittern, his pale
buff and white body nestled
in the notch of a lily leaf,
appears like a secret flower
in bloom for just this moment.

She lets her binoculars dangle
and brings her camera up instead.
The bird's golden eye watches her
and I imagine it can sense
her hushed laughter of delight
as an answering call.

CONGREGATION

We are six strangers gathered
on a gravel road in the heart
of the valley, waiting, whispering
about the flock of bald eagles
roosting in a distant stand
of cottonwoods. Then it begins:
Hunting low over the open field,
a short-eared owl streaks toward us
out of the setting sun. In this light
his face is an ochre disc, his body
mottled brown and blunt as a stogie,
long wings flashing as he passes,
tilting, listening. Near the road's edge
where shrubs ripple in the wind
he veers north, dips and zigzags
back over a shadowy fold of land,
calling his congregation to rise
from the grasses. In the late winter
chill, the air fills with their sharp barks,
the bounding predatory swoops
of fierce evening hunger.

SKY DANCE

—Portland, Oregon

Back from Mexico, the thin
male osprey climbs
through swirling spring wind
to hover over the river.

Banded tail fanned, a fish
dangling from his talons,
he undulates within
the currents. Last year's nest

perched on a power pole
below him is empty still,
but he is sure his mate
must arrive. So he dives

and swoops back up,
crooked wings rippling
as he flies loops within
the shrill echo of his cries.

A SEASON OF KILLDEER

We follow the riverbank south
past abandoned dock pilings
and a crumbling concrete pier.

At the field's edge to our west
a season of killdeer performs
routine hysterics, spooked by
an off-leash cocker spaniel.
They drag a drooping wing
across the ground, tumble
over themselves and break
into a sprint meant to lead us
all from their nesting ground.

But the rising sun is a spotlight
catching them no matter
where they turn. From home
a quarter-mile away we'd heard
their cries in the middle of
the night. The high sharp
screeches became a bubbling
trill of pure terror that seeped
through our dreams and brought
us out into this summer dawn.

NO WAKE ZONE

Workers wearing hazmat chest waders
stand hip-deep in the river's lurid waters
and pass samples to a team on the bank.
Behind them, a jet boat slams through
the river's chop, trailed upstream by laughter
and a boom box beat. The wake rocks
marker buoys as a powerboat headed
downstream slows to level its stern against
the white-tipped surge and two couples
in tandem kayaks call to each other,
angling their bows toward the spreading swells.
The workers raise their arms as if in surrender.
At the shore, a great blue heron squawks
and begins to run on the water as he lifts off.

HARVEST MOON, MANZANITA, OREGON

At night we walk the elks' path
between ocean and bay,
waves a distant hiss to the west,
cackling geese calling since dusk.

Where the ridge crests a hundred
yards east, surf pine and dune grass
release a few shadowy juncos.
Clouds chasing the full harvest
moon have gotten snagged on
Neahkahnie Mountain north of us.
It is so bright we can see a clear-cut
slope on the Coast Range ahead.

All week we have been orienting
ourselves to this new home, this new
time in our lives. I try to imagine soon
being seventy but there are so many
stars when the clouds come loose
and too much happening just inside
the forest when the wind dies down.

SIMPLE GIFTS

She sits by the window tuning
her guitar as windswept light
off the river flickers around her.

Late afternoon breeze carries
the deep thrum of a tugboat
heading back to its dock
and the fading barks of geese
flying south. She loosens
her fingers through two etudes
and a passage from "Ode to Joy."

Then she begins "Simple Gifts,"
and the melody is so familiar,
now that it is part of her practice,
I sometimes hear it in dreams.

There it is always accompanied
by her soft smile as the song
draws to a close and starts anew.

NOTES

"Chris Cagle Is Dead": Christian "Red" Cagle (1905–1942) played four years of college football at the Southwestern Louisiana Institute, then four more years at the U.S. Military Academy, where he was team captain and a three-time All-American halfback. Cagle was such an electrifying, versatile, and dominant runner-passer that he was featured on the cover of *Time* during his senior year at Army. He turned pro in 1930 and played five seasons for the New York Giants and Brooklyn Dodgers football teams. Notorious for playing without a helmet or wearing one with its chin strap loose, Cagle must have absorbed countless concussion-producing hits during his thirteen-year career. Such repeated head trauma, and the peculiar circumstances of his death at 37, when he was found at the bottom of a New York subway staircase complaining of head pain, suggest that—while Cagle may have slipped on ice or fallen down the stairs after drinking too much on the day after Christmas—he might actually have been suffering from Chronic Traumatic Encephalopathy, the degenerative brain disease now recognized as being associated with football-related head injury.

"Jules Verne at Safeco Field, Seattle, Spring 2014": As far as I know, the extraordinary French novelist did not make a vow to return from the afterlife a hundred years after his death in 1905. But I believe he would have loved to have a look at our world, especially the kinds of mechanical wonders—like Safeco Field's retractable roof—that he was inspired to imagine.

"Childe Hassam at the Oregon Coast, Summer 1904": The American Impressionist painter Frederick Childe Hassam (1859–1935), a New England native, first came to Oregon in 1904 after a period of depression and serious drinking. He spent time painting landscapes in the Cascade Mountains, the deserts east of the mountains, the city of Portland, and the north Oregon coast in and around Cannon Beach.

"Schumann in Düsseldorf, 1854": Composer Robert Schumann attempted suicide in the winter of 1854 by throwing himself off a bridge into the Rhine. Rescued, he asked to be taken to a sanatorium and died there two years later. He was 46.

CPSIA information can be obtained
at www.ICGtesting.com
Printed in the USA
LVHW092001180919
631486LV00005B/442/P